Contents

ALLAH

Allah is the Arabic word for the Supreme Being and Creator of the universe. This is used in preference to the English word 'God' except where the latter occurs in a quotation. In the English language, god can be used in the singular or plural, and as male or female, and is frequently debased or rendered meaningless by its context. The word Allah is not at all subject to such changes and uses.

THE QUR'AN

Quotations from the Qur'an used in IQRA publications are taken from: *The Message of the Qur'an, Translated and Explained* by Muhammad Asad - **MA**; *The Holy Qur'an*: Translation and Commentary by A. Yusuf Ali - **YA**; and *The Glorious Qur'an with English Translation, Introduction and Notes* by Muhammad Marmaduke Pickthall - **MP**. Quotations are cited as follows: Surah 5, ayah 43. For example, Qur'an 5:43 **YA**.

THE HADITH

Hadith in Arabic means speech, report, account. In Islam, it specifically means the deeds and sayings of the Prophet Muhammad 鐕 as recounted by his companions. All quotations from the Hadith are taken from scrupulously compiled, authenticated collections.

This symbol is the Arabic text of 'salla-llahu alayhi wassalam' which is always recited after the mention of the name of the Prophet Muhammad 鐕. It can be translated as 'May Allah bless him and give him peace.' A similar respect is accorded to all the other prophets; 鐕 (alayhi s salam) which can be translated as 'on him be peace.'

TRANSLITERATION

Diacritical marks have been omitted from the transliteration of Arabic words and phrases in order not to distract the reader.

NOTE

This publication does not claim to be more than an introduction to the subject. In addition to the recommended reading suggested here, lists of relevant material can be obtained from the IQRA Trust's database of Islamic literature.

Introduction

This book introduces some of the many Muslim travellers and explorers who lived during the Middle Ages. It tells the story of their long, sometimes difficult and dangerous journeys, and describes some of the wonderful sights they saw as they travelled through distant lands.

Some were traders, who crossed vast distances by land and sea to bring precious goods from China and India to the lands of Europe and the Middle East. Others were sent as ambassadors by Muslim rulers, to carry rich gifts as a token of respect of friendship to kings and princes who lived far away.

Some Muslim travellers were scholars, who travelled in search of knowledge. They visited colleges and universities in many parts of the world, and collected information from other travellers, as well. They compiled maps, and books full of fascinating details.

> He who travels to seek knowledge is in fact (striving) in the Path of Allah till he returns.
>
> Hadith: Tirmidhi

A few daring explorers travelled simply to see the world. They were driven by curiosity to find out all they could about the wonders and beauties of Allah's creation.

We should not forget, too, that thousands - perhaps millions - of ordinary Muslim people also made long journeys during the Middle Ages. They travelled as pilgrims, from all over the world to the city of Makkah in Arabia, as they still do now.

The Khalifah's Gifts

Khalifah Harun al-Rashid, 'Commander of the Faithful', was a rich and powerful man. He was ruler of a vast territory, which reached the borders of China. In the centre of the city of Baghdad was the magnificent palace in which he lived, with a large number of servants to look after him, and a strong bodyguard to protect him. He could call on wise courtiers to advise him whenever he wanted. His well-trained and loyal army was ready to carry out his every order and defend his lands.

But Harun al-Rashid's life, although luxurious, was not always easy. As Khalifah, he carried a heavy responsibility. It was his duty to see that the lands he ruled were governed fairly and honestly, and to ensure that the millions of people living there were undisturbed in their daily lives and protected from outside attacks. In the year 798 CE, they seemed threatened by an alliance between the other two most powerful states of that time - the kingdom of the Franks and the Byzantine Empire. How, Khalifah Harun al-Rashid wondered, could his people best be protected?

After much thought, the Khalifah decided what to do. He would make an alliance with one of his enemies. In that way they would not be able to unite against him. He feared their joint strength, but felt confident that his troops could fight off an attack by either one of them. Already Charlemagne, King of the Franks, seemed willing to consider a peace treaty. The Khalifah decided to send ambassadors to discuss terms for peace with King Charlemagne.

Baghdad was full of beautiful buildings - mosques, palaces, libraries, schools and colleges. The Khalifahs invited the best architects, artists and craftsmen to come and work in their city. Wealthy merchants also built fine houses and gardens there.

In the busy streets travellers could find shops selling goods from distant lands: silks from China, ivory and gold from Africa, spices from Malaysia, and furs, amber and jewellery from Scandinavia. In Baghdad itself, skilled workers produced fine cloth, delicate glassware, brightly decorated pottery and richly illustrated books and manuscripts.

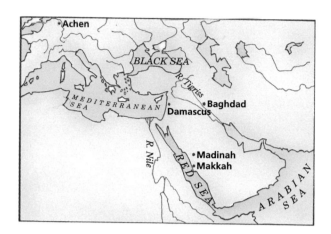

Harun al-Rashid's government was based at Baghdad, a spacious, well-planned city on the banks of the river Tigris. Baghdad was still a new city in al-Rashid's day (he reigned from 786 to 809); it had been founded by his ancestors, when they became Khalifahs, or rulers, of the Muslim world. Baghdad was also known as the 'city of peace'.

Baghdad was also famous as a centre of learning. Muslim scholars and teachers from many countries gathered there to study the Qur'an and Shari'ah, the Islamic law. Muslim scholars were famous for their learning in science, medicine, astronomy, engineering and mathematics.

An Elephant for Charlemagne

Early in 800, the ambassadors from Harun al-Rashid set off to meet King Charlemagne, to discuss the terms for peace. It was the custom, at that time, for great men to exchange valuable gifts with one another. This encouraged friendship, and showed the giver's wealth. Khalifah Harun al-Rashid took great care over the choice of a suitable gift. What was the most astonishing, unforgettable, present anyone could think of? What came from the warm, southern lands where Muslim merchants travelled, but was never seen in chilly northern Europe? What was strong and majestic, like the Khalifah himself? Harun al-Rashid decided to send an elephant to Charlemagne.

It is not known how the elephant travelled from the Khalifah's court at Baghdad to Charlemagne's capital city of Aachen, in south-western Germany. Arab merchants often made the journey by sea from eastern Mediterranean ports to the Italian trading cities of Venice or Genoa, and then northwards overland through wild and mountainous country, to do business at markets and fairs of the kingdom of the Franks. Probably, the elephant and the ambassadors travelled by the same route. However, they arrived safely in Aachen in the spring of 801, where the elephant was greeted by excited crowds as it led a procession through the streets towards Charlemagne's palace.

Charlemagne was delighted with this gift and with the other valuable presents sent by Harun al-Rashid. But the peace treaty that both rulers hoped for was never arranged. Even so, the ambassadors' journey, and the gift of the elephant, were not in vain. In the years that followed, all the links between the Khalifah's state and the kingdom of the Franks were strengthened, and Arab merchants arranged new, profitable business deals with Frankish customers. Best of all, travellers from east and west were assured of a friendly welcome in each other's lands.

Left: Historians do not know for certain what Charlemagne looked like, but this bronze statue is thought to represent him. It shows a king wearing a crown and flowing robes similar to those worn by the emperors of Ancient Rome. Charlemagne tried to revive the power and glory of the Roman rulers, and called himself 'Holy Roman Emperor.'

The teachings of Khalifah Harun al-Rashid's Islamic faith led him to prefer peace to war. To avoid bloodshed, he made an alliance with Charlemagne and sent him many gifts, including brilliantly coloured silk, perfumes, a golden bowl and jug, chessmen made of ivory, a tent with glossy silken curtains, and a marvellous clock, which signalled the hours by dropping bronze balls into a bowl, while doors opened to reveal miniature figures of knights on horseback. To Charlemagne's courtiers, this clock appeared to work by magic, but it was, in fact, powered by water, and was designed to display the inventiveness and skills of the Khalifah's Muslim craftsmen, as well as to entertain. The ambassadors also presented Charlemagne with a magnificent robe, with the words 'There is only One God' embroidered on it in Arabic.

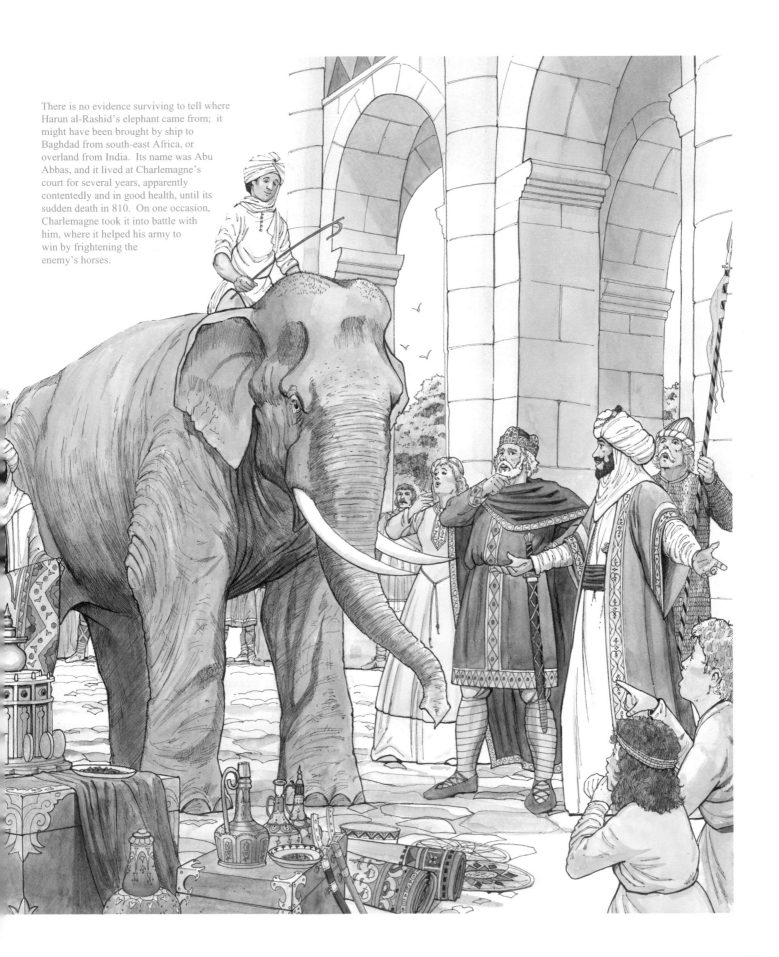

There is no evidence surviving to tell where Harun al-Rashid's elephant came from; it might have been brought by ship to Baghdad from south-east Africa, or overland from India. Its name was Abu Abbas, and it lived at Charlemagne's court for several years, apparently contentedly and in good health, until its sudden death in 810. On one occasion, Charlemagne took it into battle with him, where it helped his army to win by frightening the enemy's horses.

Travelling North

On 21 June in the year 921, a party of travellers set out from Baghdad, at the centre of the Muslim world. They were ambassadors from Khalifah al-Muqtadir to the court of the King of Slavs who ruled over a vast, snow-covered kingdom in what is now northern Russia.

The previous year, he had written to the Khalifah, asking him to send someone to teach his people all about Islam and to help build a mosque where Muslims could meet and pray. Naturally, the Khalifah in Baghdad was eager to help so he asked Nadhir al-Harami, a wise and scholarly man, to travel to the kingdom of the Slavs with a group of companions, and to spread the teachings of the Qur'an to everyone he met on his journey.

Baghdad was a very long way - over 1,500 km - from the lands where the Slav king ruled. How did the Slavs know about the Khalifah, his beautiful city, and the learned men who lived there? The answer is, through trade. Muslim merchants frequently braved harsh, wintry weather conditions to travel to the northern lands where Slav and Viking tribes lived. A network of trade routes had developed, which passed through dense forests and along icy rivers.

We know about the north-south trade because objects made by Muslim craftsmen living and working in Egypt, Spain, Turkey and Persia have been found by archaeologists excavating sites in Scandinavia and northern Russia, just as goods made by Slav and Viking craftsmen have been found at sites in Middle Eastern lands. By sending al-Harami and his companions to meet the King of the Slavs, the Khalifah hoped to turn these trading links into something deeper and more important - brotherhood in Islam.

Goods traded between Muslim and Viking merchants. Objects like these have been discovered by archaeologists at sites in Scandinavia and in Islamic countries of the Middle East.

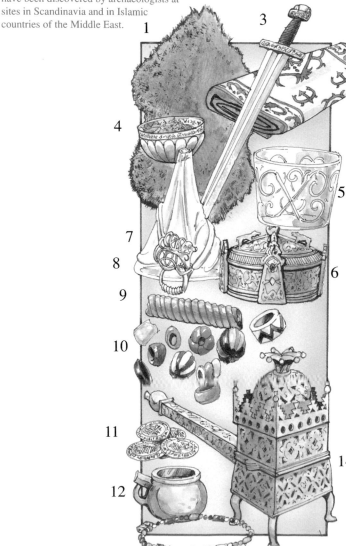

1. Furs from animals trapped in northern forests.

2. Silks from China.

3. Viking swords.

4. Spices from India and the East Indies.

5. Glassware from the Rhineland (Germany).

6. Viking box-shaped brooch, worn by women.

7. Glassware from Baghdad, with decorations in Arabic script.

8. Viking silver brooch.

9. Glass from northern Italy. Tubes like this were used to make the next item.

10. Viking glass beads.

11. Silver coins from the Viking countries in the Middle East.

12. Glazed pottery cup, from Persia.

13. Viking silver necklace.

14. Bronze brazier (a hollow box, where charcoal or incense could be burned). The sides are pierced with holes to allow air to enter, and smoke or fumes to escape. Made in Baghdad.

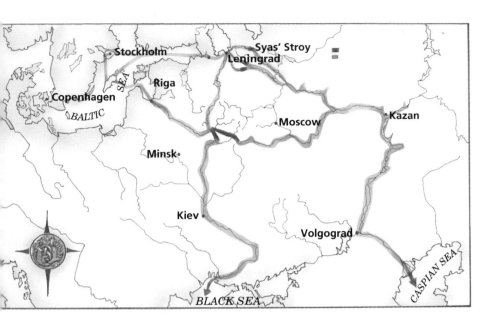

Among the Vikings

Among those who went with the Khalifah's ambassador on his journey to the north was Ibn Fadlan, a very observant secretary. He wrote a diary of his travels, full of interesting descriptions of the countryside they passed through, the terrible cold they endured, and the different peoples they met. Without Ibn Fadlan's account, we would know very little of the expedition, or what life was like at that time (the mid-10th century) in the places he visited.

Ibn Fadlan gives vivid pictures of the differing ways of life he saw on his travels. He was fascinated to discover, for example, that the Oghuz Turks, who lived in the lands to the north of the Caspian Sea, made their homes in tents (called yurts), which consisted of heavy felt, arranged over a network of poles. The Oghuz were nomads, and wandered over a wide area, seeking grazing land for their flocks and herds. They had few possessions, and their simple lifestyle was a great contrast to the comfortable city conditions that Ibn Fadlan was used to. As a result of their contacts with Muslim travellers and traders, the Oghuz people eventually became faithful followers of Islam.

Ibn Fadlan has also left us very dramatic descriptions of certain Viking customs. The Vikings or 'Rus', as he called them, lived in the far north of Russia and in the Scandinavian lands. He reported that they were brave, strong and warlike, skilled craftsmen, and shrewd traders. The illustration opposite is based on Ibn Fadlan's eye-witness account of the funeral and cremation of a Viking warrior chief. Instead of the simple burial Ibn Fadlan was used to, he was shocked and saddened to see the customs of the Vikings.

Ibn Fadlan and his companions saw many unfamiliar sights during the time they spent travelling among the Viking peoples. Ibn Fadlan's detailed descriptions of Viking customs and ceremonies, preserved in the report he wrote for the Khalifah back home in Baghdad, form a very valuable record which is still consulted by archaeologists and historians today.

Without Ibn Fadlan's careful observations, little would be known, for example, about Viking cremation customs, since no evidence, apart from a few charred remains, would survive after the fire.

According to Islamic tradition, dead Muslims are washed and shrouded with great care and respect. Then prayers are said for them, and they are quietly buried in a simple grave. Ibn Fadlan, who was a Muslim, was therefore horrified at the way the Vikings treated their dead.

At a Viking funeral, a dead warrior's nearest male relative was chief mourner. It was his duty to set fire to the coffin-ship, with its cargo of the dead man and his possessions: treasures, horses, hunting-dogs and slaves. The funeral bonfire was kindled by throwing lighted sticks at the burial ship, which was surrounded by straw and dry kindling. To show how upset he was, the chief mourner threw off all his clothes, and appeared half-mad with grief.

Travellers' Tales

In the 10th century, Baghdad was a city where many men of knowledge lived, scholars studied all the books of learning which they could find, and investigated the laws of Allah's creation.

How curious and eager these men must have been to hear news of Ibn Fadlan's travels. Through him, they heard of the effects of sub-zero temperatures: seas and rivers turned to ice, trees and buildings cracked apart, and once even his own beard, damp with steam, froze solid as he made his way back to his lodgings from the bath-house. Information like this helped the scientists in Baghdad to understand the created world and in particular the properties of different materials such as water, wood and stone.

Ibn Fadlan's diary is very entertaining, even today, over 1,000 years after it was written. If he spoke as well as he wrote, he must have been an amusing story-teller and a popular guest. Here he describes, for example, how funny the travellers looked as they wrapped themselves up in layers of clothing to keep warm: 'Each of us wore a tunic, and over that a caftan, and over that a sheepskin robe, and over that a felt cloak, and over that a burnous - after which, only our eyes showed. We also wore a pair of ordinary trousers and a pair of fur-lined ones, slippers, light boots and, over those more boots, so that each of us, on climbing on his camel, found he could hardly move ...'

On his return to Baghdad, Ibn Fadlan had many stories to tell about the people he had seen and the countries he had visited on his long journey. His listeners, who were used to a hot, dry climate, were astonished to learn of the bitterly cold weather conditions in the northern lands.

This is one of the stories that Ibn Fadlan told about the sub-zero temperatures that people living north of the Caspian Sea had to endure: 'I was told that two men had set out with a dozen camels, intending to load them with wood from the forest, but they forgot to take kindling and steel (for striking sparks to light a fire) with them. They had to spend the night without any fire, and by morning, they and their camels were dead ...'

Ibn Fadlan's audience not only included scholars and scientists but also Baghdad merchants, eager for news of goods for sale, prices paid and bargains struck. They admired the rare and beautiful objects Ibn Fadlan and his companions brought back from their travels to the icy north.

Here is how Ibn Fadlan described the Viking people who came to meet the Muslim ambassadors. 'I have never seen men so beautiful as they were - they were like palm trees. They are fair and their skin is white and red ... Each of them has an axe, a broadsword, and a knife. All the women wear an enormous kind of box (or brooch) of iron, silver, copper, gold or wood, depending on the wealth of their husband.'

Travellers like Ibn Fadlan, soldiers, and merchants purchased these swords and brooches, which were often beautifully made by craftsmen, and took them home to Baghdad.

The Kingdom of Sicily

King Roger of Sicily was well known for his energy and enthusiasm. One writer remarked that King Roger 'accomplished more in his sleep than most kings did when they were awake'. After only a few years as king, Roger was respected throughout the Mediterranean world for the skill with which he governed his kingdom, as well as for his knowledge and learning.

Now, in 1138, he was determined to make a start on his most ambitious project yet. He wanted to appoint a team of scholars to draw a map which would show the whole of the known world, based on scientific measurement and careful observation. No one had ever dared to suggest anything so difficult and complicated before. King Roger already possessed an excellent library, and had many learned men among his courtiers, but now he needed an expert geographer to help him.

King Roger invited the famous Arab scholar, al-Idrisi, to leave his home town in Ceuta, North Africa, and come and live in Palermo, to supervise the preparation of the great world map.

Between them, King Roger and al-Idrisi drew up a plan of study. Scholars working in the palace library, and travelling to consult books and charts in other collections if necessary, were told to summarise all that was already known about the surface of the earth. Other researchers were instructed to ask travellers and sailors arriving in Sicilian ports from overseas about all the countries they had visited. Al-Idrisi also sent out teams of investigators, accompanied by artists and map-makers, to report back on various distant lands. This research took over 15 years to complete. According to al-Idrisi, hardly a day passed without King Roger visiting the library to check on the progress of the work.

King Roger gave orders that all sailors arriving in Sicilian ports should be questioned about the countries they had visited and the sights they had seen on their voyages. Al-Idrisi and his team of scholars collected a great deal of information from these eye-witness accounts of distant lands, and used it to help them compile their map of the world.

By comparing the sailors' accounts of their journeys with the writings of earlier geographers and scientists, they hoped to get a more accurate picture of the climate, vegetation, buildings, crops and civilizations of different countries, as well as an estimate of the distance between one port or city and another.

From 831-1101, Sicily had been ruled by Muslim governors, who had built irrigation systems, including dams, reservoirs, and water-towers. These enabled luxury crops, such as oranges and lemons, sugar, cotton, dates and rice, to be grown on the island. The Muslim governors also encouraged the mining and fishing industries. By King Roger's day, Sicily was a thriving, prosperous kingdom. It lay at the crossroads of several important land and sea routes linking countries bordering the Mediterranean Sea.

Sicilian ports were crowded with ships from many lands: solid, ocean-going 'cogs' from northern Europe, sleek galleys from Spain and Italy, warships from Byzantium and cargo vessels of all shapes and sizes from North Africa, Cyprus, Greece and Palestine. The inhabitants of Sicily also came from many different countries, but lived peacefully together, despite their different languages, customs and faiths. Even Sicilian architecture was a mixture of eastern and western styles.

A Map of the World

King Roger chose al-Idrisi to supervise his great map because Muslim geographers were renowned for their skills and their knowledge, and also for their scientific approach. They had a great tradition of scientific learning to build on.

The Prophet Muhammad ﷺ valued knowledge highly. To encourage Muslims to study and learn about Allah's creation, he said, 'If anyone travels on a road in search of knowledge, Allah will cause him to travel on one of the roads of Paradise', and so for centuries, Muslim astronomers, mathematicians and scientists had studied problems of measurement, navigation and geometry. They learned how to study living things and people scientifically. The Qur'an too, which formed the basis of Islamic education, contains many references to animal biology, weather, geology and astronomy, and was far in advance of human scientific knowledge at the time of its revelation.

When the work was completed, al-Idrisi presented the map, engraved on a large silver disc, and a long, very detailed book, containing a great deal of information about many different countries. This is part of his description of Britain: '... there are flourishing towns, high mountains, great rivers and plains. The country is most fertile; its inhabitants are brave, active and enterprising, but all is in the grip of perpetual winter.'

King Roger and al-Idrisi interviewed many Muslim travellers while compiling their map. These travellers and others like them journeyed in every direction - trading, building mosques and teaching Islam. Some of their trade routes and mosques are used to this day.

King Roger was one of the best-educated rulers of his time. He encouraged Muslim and Christian scholars to come to his court, and was keenly interested in their discoveries. Al-Idrisi was full of praise for the King's intellect: 'In mathematics as in politics,' he wrote, 'the extent of his (King Roger's) learning cannot be described. Nor is there any limit to his knowledge of the sciences, so deeply and wisely has he studied them...'

Al-Idrisi hoped that his silver map would last longer than one drawn on parchment. Unfortunately, it was destroyed during a rebellion in 1160. But al-Idrisi's Arabic text, which described the silver map in detail, and contained over 100 smaller maps, did survive, and was consulted by Muslim scholars and travellers for many years. It was known as 'The Delight of One who wishes to Traverse the Regions of the World'.

A circular Arabic map based on al-Idrisi's lost silver disc. On it you can clearly see the Mediterranean Sea, the Arabian peninsula, the Nile delta and a huge southern continent (based on Africa) occupying the lower section of the map.

Al-Idrisi drew his map with Africa at the top. We turned it for you to recognise the places more easily. So now the Arabic writing is upside down.

King Roger admires the map prepared by al-Idrisi and his team. It was engraved on to the surface of a huge, silver disc, about two metres in diameter and weighing over 150 kg.

21

Jerusalem

Jerusalem is a special city for Jews, Christians and Muslims. Jewish people remember it as the place where the Prophet Sulayman 鑑 (Solomon) built a great temple; Christians remember it as the city where Isa 鑑 (Jesus) preached; and Muslims remember it as the place where the Prophet Muhammad 鑑 made a miraculous journey.

Since 638 when it was captured by Umar, the second Khalifah, Jerusalem had been governed by the Islamic khilafah (caliphate). As a result of this rule, Christians and Muslims were able to live there peacefully together. Members of each faith as 'People of the Book' were free to worship as they pleased, and the city had many beautiful mosques, churches and synagogues. Jewish, Christian and Muslim travellers visited the city, to pray there and to see the fine houses belonging to wealthy merchants and scholars, and the noisy, busy markets and workshops.

In the 11th century, control over the Islamic territories in the Middle East passed from the Arab Khalifahs of Baghdad to a new dynasty of rulers, the Seljuks. They were of Turkish origin, and had accepted Islam. In 1071 they defeated the armies of the Byzantine empire at the battle of Manzikert, and took control of Turkey.

The rulers of Europe were alarmed by this victory. They feared that the Seljuks might continue their expansion westwards. But from the Seljuks' point of view, they were only protecting their lands from the threat of attack by the Byzantines. Then in 1095, Pope Urban, the spiritual leader of western Christians, took action and declared a crusade, or holy war, against the Muslim rulers of Jerusalem. He called on Christian soldiers to travel to Palestine, and fight until the city was in Christian hands.

Jerusalem was a place of pilgrimage for people of Jewish, Christian and Muslim faiths. Parties of believers would come from distant lands, often facing hardship and danger on their journeys. Even during the time of the crusades, when the area round Jerusalem became a battleground, pilgrims still risked the journey, out of devotion to their faith.

Military commanders on both sides during the crusades (see next page) issued safe-conducts to pilgrims, asking for them to be protected as they travelled through enemy territory. These were respected by Muslim and Christian soldiers alike. Here is one example, issued by Tancred, a Christian leader, in 1112: 'This is a revered knight of the Franks who had completed the holy pilgrimage and is now on his way back to his country ... Treat him well.'

On his journey through Palestine, the knight met Usamah Ibn Munqidh, an Arab gentleman enrolled in the Muslim army. Usamah praised the knight's courage (he had heard of his brave exploits in battle, before he became a pilgrim), and, even though they were on opposing sides in the conflict, thanked Allah for it. In his memoirs Usamah wrote, 'Exalted be Allah who can do what He pleases.'

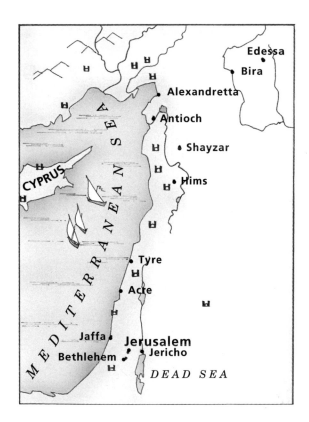

War in the East

The first crusade began in 1086, and for the next 200 years the attacks on Palestine continued. Kings and princes from England, France, Germany and elsewhere in Europe, together with their best fighting men, launched a series of attacks on the most important towns and cities, and built massive castles to keep watch over any land they managed to seize. In 1099, Christian forces captured Jerusalem, and disgracefully massacred the people living there - men, women and even children.

The defending armies fought back and there were many casualties on both sides. Jerusalem was finally recaptured by the great Muslim leader Saladin in 1187, and the defeated crusader army sailed away in 1191.

Military architects working for Muslim and Christian army commanders at the time of the crusades designed and built some magnificent castles. This illustration shows the Muslim castle of Krak des Chevaliers in Syria.

Fortunately, the old, tolerant way of life was not completely destroyed by the crusades. Travellers to Palestine described how, during pauses in the fighting, soldiers would stage playful mock battles, or even join in children's games. The Muslim troops were taught by their religion not to harm women, children or the elderly, not to cut down fruit-bearing trees, nor to destroy any place where people were living or to slaughter sheep or camels, except for food. Even bees and their hives were to be kept safe.

The important cities of Palestine were also fortified by massive walls, with watch-towers and strong gatehouses. The only way to capture these well-defended cities and castles was by a siege; an enemy army would surround a castle or city and try to batter down its walls while, at the same time, preventing supplies of fresh food and armaments from reaching it. The besieged inhabitants were often faced with an awful choice between starvation and surrender.

Muslim and Christian soldiers playing chess, a
game which originated in Islamic lands, and later spread to
Europe, where it became very popular among the upper classes during
the Middle Ages. There are many recorded instances of Muslim and
Christian co-operation during the years of the crusades. For example,
when the English king, Richard the Lionheart, lay sick in bed with a fever,
Saladin, the Muslim leader, sent him a present of peaches, pears and snow
(to make cooling drinks) from the upper slopes of Mount Hermon.

In Europe, soldiers did not usually wear extra layers of clothing on top of
their armour. But in the warm climate of Palestine, metal rings and plates
grew blisteringly hot under the sun. So Christian soldiers copied the
Muslim habit of wearing a light robe over their armour, perhaps to stop the
armour becoming hot. And Christians living in Palestine soon learned to
follow the Muslim practice of covering their heads and wearing long, loose
clothing, which was cooler, cleaner and thus more comfortable in the heat.

The Silk Route

Throughout the Middle Ages, but especially during the 12th, 13th and early 14th centuries, there was a flourishing long-distance trade between Europe and the Far East. Merchants from Christian and Islamic lands undertook long and exhausting journeys overland to the great trading posts of Bukhara, Tashkent and Samarkand in Central Asia, or even further afield to the fabulously wealthy Chinese cities of Sian and Hangchow. There were also important trading colonies along the shores of the Black Sea, where merchants met to haggle over prices and search for bargains.

What did these merchants carry with them on their journeys? What did they buy and sell? European merchants wanted to buy two main types of goods from producers in the Far East: silks and spices. Other goods, such as porcelain, gold and precious stones, were also imported from eastern lands, but the silk trade, in particular, was so important that one of the most frequently-used trackways for travellers to China became known as the 'Silk Route' as early as Roman times. Silk came from 'factories' in China, where the local people had perfected the art of rearing silkworms and unravelling the fine thread from their cocoons.

Spices came from India and the islands to the east, along with pearls from the Indian Ocean, and sapphires and rubies from Sri Lanka and Burma. The supply of all these goods was largely controlled by Arab and Indian merchants.

In return, Mediterranean and Middle Eastern countries exported glassware, pottery, fine metalwork, scientific instruments and woollen cloth. The peoples who lived along the Silk Route also made goods to sell. Beautiful carpets, dyed in glowing colours, were made by villagers in Turkey and Central Asia, and purchased by merchants from both east and west.

All the beautiful and valuable objects shown on these pages were traded between Muslim merchants from the Middle East and craftsmen and merchants from China and the Far East. It was a two-way trade: pottery, glassware, carpets and metalwork from the west were exported to China, and fine porcelain (which only the Chinese knew how to make), silks, jewels and spices were brought back to Europe and the Middle East.

This map shows the main trade routes between the eastern Mediterranean area and the fabulously wealthy cities of China and the East Indies. Merchants travelled overland across Asia, or by sea to India and the lands beyond.

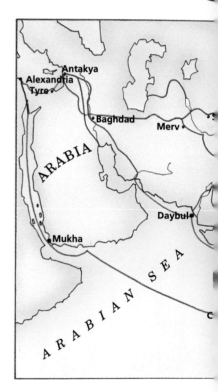

7. Decorated Egyptian pottery bowl. 13th century.

8. Chinese silk with a woven pattern, known as brocade.

9. Chinese celadon (see 13) porcelain bowl.

10. Chinese porcelain dish with spout.

11. Pottery vase from Persia.

12. Chinese earthenware vase.

13. Chinese celadon (greenish glaze) bowl and dish.

14. Astrolabe from Cordoba in Muslim Spain. Used for navigation by means of the stars.

15. Carpet from Turkey. 14th century.

16. Egyptian copper bowl with inlaid decoration.

17. Persian silver and gold casket. 14th century.

18. Mongol earrings.

19. Egyptian water jug, made of rock crystal.

20. Syrian glass beaker, decorated with gilt and enamel. c.1260.

21. Venetian glass, decorated with enamel. c.1280.

22. Pottery bowls from Persia.

1

1. Pottery dish with a metallic sheen, late 12th century, Iran.

2. Egyptian decorated earthenware jar.

3. Fine porcelain from China.

4. 'Chi-chou' porcelain from China. This is a teapot, designed to look like a bundle of cloth.

5. Woven silk, in a style typical of both the Byzantine Empire and Iran, 11th century.

6. Gold 'safe-conduct' tablet, given to foreign travellers in China by the Emperor. The tablet proved to the Chinese people (particularly soldiers, or government officials) that the traveller who carried it was under the Emperor's protection.

15

18

16

17

19

20

21

22

11

12

13

Turfan

shgar

Khotan

Xi'an

Canton

Port of Ganges

Rangoon

5

8

6

9

10

3

4

7

Dangerous Journeys

The journey along the Silk Route could be difficult and dangerous. It passed through several extremes of climate, from the hot, dry, desert lands of the Middle East, across the snowy mountains of Armenia and Azerbaijan, to the windswept plains of Central Asia, where the night-time temperatures fell below freezing for nine months of the year. The most terrifying stage of the journey was crossing the Gobi Desert. There, rocks and posts marking the way could easily be hidden by sudden sandstorms, leaving travellers stranded in the wilderness.

There was danger, too, from disease, hunger and thirst. Travellers took emergency supplies of food and water with them, but also had to rely on buying provisions for themselves and fodder for their animals from villages or nomad encampments along the way. Muslim travellers had faith that Allah would protect them on their journeys, but also made careful plans. The Prophet Muhammad ﷺ taught: 'Trust in Allah for everything, but tie your camel first!'

Travellers might be attacked by highway robbers, bandits or enemy soldiers. Merchants travelled in convoys for safety, with armed guards and local guides to protect them.

Merchants and other travellers found safety in the great market towns, such as Samarkand and Bukhara, which grew up along the most important trading routes. There, people from many lands mingled in the crowded bazaars, or shared the hospitality of the noisy, busy rest-houses for travellers.

A caravanserai on the Silk Route. Travellers could stop and rest at inns like these, where they could purchase food and drink, and also fodder and a warm shelter for their packhorses and camels. Travelling merchants traded with one another, or exchanged information on the state of the roads, the weather conditions or even the presence of bandits and robbers in the area.

Caravanserais provided a welcome opportunity for rest and relaxation after weeks of travelling through harsh and sometimes hostile territory. Travellers could sleep on rugs or mattresses in heated rooms, instead of on the hard earth, or in a draughty tent.
Food served in caravanserais was simple - mutton stew, perhaps, or millet porridge. To drink, there might be ewe's or mare's milk, or black tea with butter floating on top..

Objects from areas where the Mongol peoples lived. Since the Mongols spent all their lives on the move, following their herds as they sought fresh grazing, their goods had to be easily transportable. They made special containers for carrying fragile or precious objects.

1. Transport chest, beautifully carved out of wood. It was designed to carry fragile Chinese porcelain.

2. Metal objects were also prized, because they were less likely to break while being carried around. This is a samovar, for heating water and brewing tea. The Mongols purchased tea from Chinese merchants.

3. Wood and leather carrying cases for porcelain bowls.

Welcome Visitors

Even though the Silk Route overland across Asia was closed after 1368, goods from the Far East still reached European markets during the later 14th and 15th centuries. This was largely due to the skill and enterprise of Arab and Indian merchants, who had long ago established a network of sea routes from the Spice Islands (modern Malaysia, Java and Sumatra) around the coast of India and along the Arabian Gulf. Goods were then unloaded at the busy port of Basrah, and carried by camel train to seaports on the south-eastern Mediterranean coast.

An alternative route used ships to ferry goods through the Red Sea. They were then taken overland to Alexandria, the most important trading city in Egypt, and loaded once more on to ships, to be carried westwards on swift cargo vessels to ports in Italy, France and Spain.

Spices were a valuable, and very profitable commodity. They were highly prized in Europe and in the Middle East because they added variety to monotonous dishes of stewed mutton, dried peas, or barley broth. They covered up the taste of stale meat or fish, and added delicious flavours of their own when cooked with fine flour, nuts, eggs and honey to make delicacies such as gingerbread or cinnamon wafers.

Venice, in northern Italy, was a great centre of the spice trade. Not surprisingly, Venetian merchants established close friendships and partnerships with well-travelled traders and explorers from Muslim lands. And, after they had concluded their business deals, many Venetian merchants must have enjoyed listening to the tales told by their Muslim visitors, recounting their adventures in the lands of silks and spices.

A wealthy merchant greets a party of Muslim travellers who have arrived in Venice with rare and exotic goods to sell. He is accompanied by his business partners and his young clerk, who is ready to record details of the day's business on the sheets of parchment he is holding.

The ground floor of a Venetian merchant's house was devoted to trade. As well as the landing stage outside, there would be an imposing courtyard and entrance hall, where visitors could be welcomed. There were also storerooms, a strong-room and a counting house (like an office). The courtyard would probably also contain a well, to collect rainwater, which was filtered before drinking, and a garden where herbs and flowers were grown. These were used in cooking, and to make scents and medicines.

The merchant and his family lived on the upper floors of the house, which were often reached by a staircase leading up from the courtyard. These private rooms were often very luxuriously furnished and beautifully decorated.

Venice was built around a network of canals, which served the city almost like streets. Wealthy merchants built their great houses (known as palaces) along the banks of the Grand Canal, with a landing stage, where boats could be moored, in front of the main entrance.

Setting Out

'It is plain to any man of intelligence that this sheikh is the traveller of our time, and if anyone were to call him the greatest traveller the Muslim world has ever known, they would not be exaggerating.' This is how Ibn Juzayy, private secretary to the sultan of Fez, in Morocco, described Ibn Battutah, who had spent the past 28 years travelling, and whose journeys covered over 120,000 km. Ibn Juzayy had just finished copying out the notes dictated to him by Ibn Battutah, in which he gave a full account of his travels, and of the people and places he had seen. Ibn Juzayy's book was written over 600 years ago, in 1363, but has survived, been translated into many languages, and can still be read today.

Ibn Battutah was born in Tangier, a busy Moroccan city on the North African coast. His family was wealthy, and he received a good education. He was trained in the Islamic law, and planned to make a career as a qadi, or judge. But in 1325 when he was 22 years old, Ibn Battutah decided to leave home and go on Hajj (pilgrimage to the city of Makkah) as all Muslims must make a firm intention to do at some time during their lives.

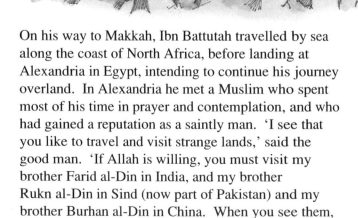

On his way to Makkah, Ibn Battutah travelled by sea along the coast of North Africa, before landing at Alexandria in Egypt, intending to continue his journey overland. In Alexandria he met a Muslim who spent most of his time in prayer and contemplation, and who had gained a reputation as a saintly man. 'I see that you like to travel and visit strange lands,' said the good man. 'If Allah is willing, you must visit my brother Farid al-Din in India, and my brother Rukn al-Din in Sind (now part of Pakistan) and my brother Burhan al-Din in China. When you see them, greet them for me.'

Ibn Battutah was a tireless traveller. The maps on this page show the various stages in his first great journey, Map 1 shows the extent of his travels in North and East Africa as well as Arabia and the Middle East. Each of the numbered squares shows the area covered by one of the smaller maps.

Map 2 shows the first stages of his journey, from Tangier along the North African coast.

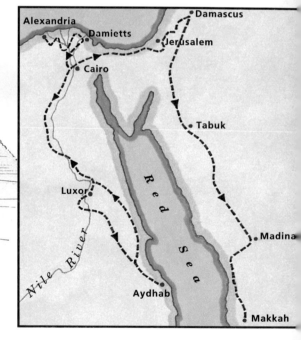

Map 3 shows how he went on through the countries bordering the Red Sea.

Map 4 shows how Ibn Battutah left Makkah and Madinah and journeyed eastwards, sometimes doubling back on his tracks, until he reached Tabriz, an important trading city not far from the Black Sea.

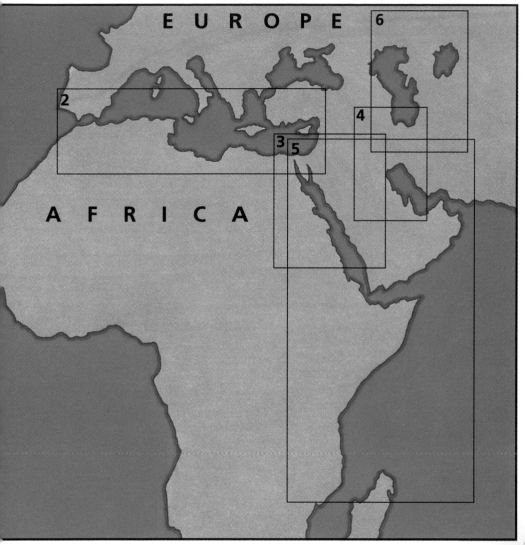

E U R O P E

A F R I C A

2

3 5 4 6

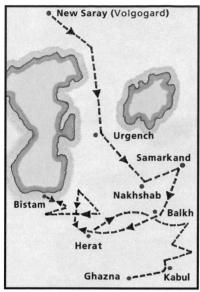

New Saray (Volgogard)

Urgench

Samarkand

Bistam

Nakhshab

Balkh

Herat

Ghazna

Kabul

Map 6. Some time shortly afterwards (we are not quite sure when), Ibn Battutah set off again north-eastwards, and travelled to the trading station at New Serai, on the banks of the Volga river. From there, he journeyed through wild and mountainous countryside to Afghanistan, passing through the splendid cities of Bukhara and Samarkand. These great journeys - from Morocco to the foothills of the Himalayas - took Ibn Battutah over 10 years to accomplish.

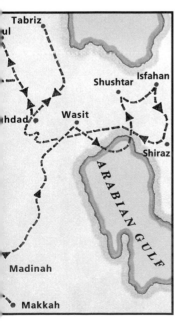

Tabriz

ul

Shushtar

Isfahan

hdad

Wasit

Shiraz

ARABIAN GULF

Madinah

Makkah

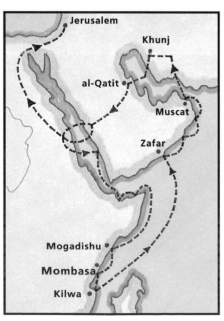

Jerusalem

Khunj

al-Qatit

Muscat

Zafar

Mogadishu

Mombasa

Kilwa

Map 5: He then returned to Arabia, and this time journeyed southwards, sailing down the Red Sea and along the eastern coast of Africa. He returned to Makkah via the ports on the southern coast of the Arabian peninsula, and along the Arabian Gulf.

A Change of Plan

Ibn Battutah continued his journey towards Makkah, but he could not forget the words spoken by the man in Alexandria. 'I was astonished at this speech,' he remembered, as he dictated his book to Ibn Juzayy, '... and the desire to go to those countries was planted in my mind. I never ceased to travel until I had met the three men that he (the saintly man) had named, and given them his greeting.'

First of all Ibn Battutah had to complete his pilgrimage. After several delays and detours, including a visit to Palestine, he reached Arabia in 1326. He travelled to Madinah, to visit the mosque of the Prophet Muhammad* and then on to Makkah, where he joined other pilgrims from Muslim countries all over the world. He had originally intended to return to his home in Tangier when his pilgrimage was over, but now his plans had changed. He set off eastwards, in search of the three Muslim brothers, who lived in far-off lands.

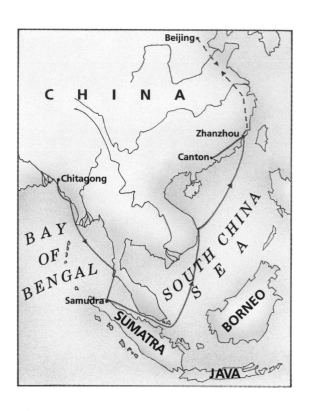

The maps on these pages show the various stages in Ibn Battutah's journeys to India and China. He set off towards India in 1333 (map 1) and spent several years living in Delhi, at the court of a powerful sultan.

After several adventures while still in the sultan's service, he decided to set out again, and headed for China. He travelled by sea, along the coasts of present-day Bangladesh, Burma, Malaysia and Vietnam (map 2). He was very impressed by the wealthy Chinese cities, and stayed there for several years.

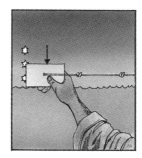

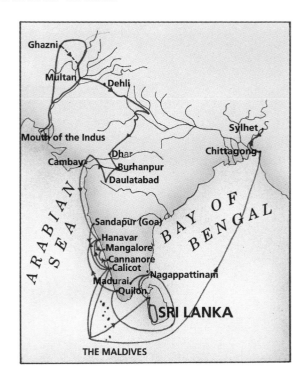

On board ship, Ibn Battutah learned many skills from the Arab sailors, including how to navigate, using a device known as a 'kamal' (it means 'guiding line'). This helped to fix a ship's position in relation to the North Star, and told the sailors how far east or west they had travelled since losing sight of land. Muslim travellers, used to crossing vast, featureless deserts and oceans, were the first to develop several ingenious ways of navigating by means of the stars.

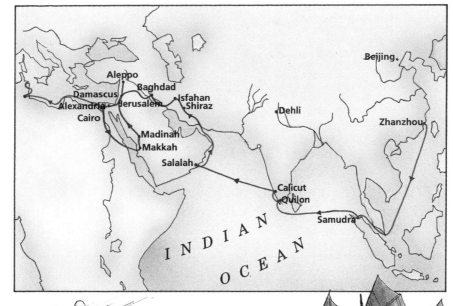

This map shows Ibn Battutah's return journey, again by sea, until he reached Arabia. He then travelled overland (by a roundabout route) until he reached Alexandria, where he boarded a ship which took him to his home town of Tangier. He arrived there in 1349, almost 25 years after first leaving his native city.

On the overland stage of his journey to China, Ibn Battutah travelled on horseback. He rode a sturdy pony, bred by the Mongols.

On his journey to China, Ibn Battutah would have seen many junks (three-masted ships like the one shown here) sailing down rivers or between coastal ports, heavily laden with cargo.

...dia, kings and princes travelled on canopied seats ...he backs of specially trained elephants. Ibn ...utah visited one Indian sultan who used to send an ...hant into the city streets, loaded with an automatic ...pult which scattered gold and silver coins among ...eople.

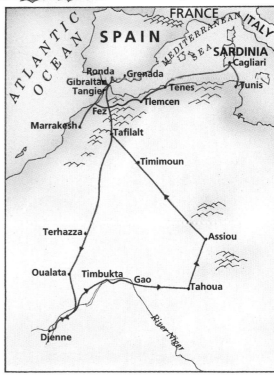

Here is Ibn Battutah's last major journey, inland from Tangier across the Sahara to the kingdom of Mali and the Niger river.

...he travelled to Baghdad, the former capital of the Muslim ...rld, he was saddened to see the destruction caused by the ...ongol attack in 1258. These pagan Mongols tribes had fought ...ir way westwards from their homelands around the shores of ...ke Baikal. They now controlled many of the former Muslim ...ritories to the east of Baghdad and had killed local rulers, ...fire to cities, and fought the Muslim troops. They did, ...wever, allow the farmers and peasants to continue with their ...eryday lives and did not stop them practising their Islamic ...th. They also allowed Muslim merchants to travel along ...ll-known trade routes between Europe and the Far East. ...a result, by the 14th century, many Mongol chieftains and ...ir subjects had accepted Islam. Ibn Battutah spent the next ...v years travelling through Central Asia in the company of ...e Mongols, and has left us detailed descriptions of their ...y of life.

India and China

Ibn Battutah returned to Makkah, but could not settle down. He decided to visit India and set off following the overland route, through Turkey and Afghanistan. With his companions he travelled in covered wagons, which he found very comfortable. As he described them to Ibn Juzayy, they had windows protected by a screen: 'The person inside ... can see without being seen, and can spend his time as he likes, sleeping or eating or reading or writing while he is travelling...'

Eventually Ibn Battutah reached Delhi and made his way to the magnificent palace where the sultan lived. It was surrounded by armed guards, flute players and trumpeters, who played a fanfare when anyone important arrived. The sultan held court every day, surrounded by 200 soldiers, 60 horses and 50 elephants. Ibn Battutah was soon invited to stay at the sultan's palace and, because of his Islamic legal training, served as a judge in the Islamic Shari'ah courts.

He remained in Delhi for several years, but resumed his travels in 1342, when he was sent by the sultan as an ambassador to the Great Khan, the Mongol ruler of China. Unfortunately, Ibn Battutah's plans to reach China were wrecked by a series of disasters, and after many adventures, he reached the Maldive Islands in the Indian Ocean. Once again, he was asked to serve as a judge in the Islamic courts, and did so, until he again grew restless, and resumed his travels.
He sailed to Sri Lanka, Burma and Sumatra, and then finally to China.

Ibn Battutah explored the Chinese countryside, and was amazed by the prosperity of the Chinese cities. But after a chance meeting with Muslim merchants who also came from Morocco, he began to feel homesick, and started on the long journey westwards by sea.

Ibn Battutah entertaining his fellow-passengers on board an Arab cargo ship.

Story-tellers, like Ibn Battutah, were very welcome company on long voyages. Ibn Battutah's companions on board ship must have been astonished by his descriptions of life in the far-away places he had visited, and amused by his stories of how he had escaped from difficult and dangerous situations.

There were no passenger ships in Ibn Battutah's time. Travellers had to find space to eat and sleep in the crowded holds of cargo ships, among bales of cloth, sacks of grain and jars of oil.

Journeys by sailing ship were long and slow. Life on board could be tedious, especially if the ship was becalmed. There was nothing to look at except the wide ocean, and nothing much to do, except wait for the wind to blow.

Food on board ship was simple and monotonous. Travellers carried their own supplies of dry bread or biscuits, and fresh or dried fruit (dates, raisins, apples and apricots). The sailors trailed baited lines overboard, in the hope of catching fish. On some long journeys, chickens in coops were carried on board with, perhaps, one or two goats, to provide fresh eggs and milk.

The Greatest Traveller

Ibn Battutah survived many accidents and adventures in the course of his travels. He says, for example, that during the long sea voyage home from China he passed an island which seemed suddenly to rise up into the air. The sailors who were with him swore they had also witnessed this marvel, and suggested that the island might not have been dry land at all, but the mythical giant bird known as the 'Roc', which was believed to inhabit the southern seas, and which the passing ship had disturbed while it was asleep.

Even so, his description of his final journey, across the Sahara desert to the African kingdoms such as Mali, is full of details that can be confirmed from the writings of later travellers. Wherever he travelled in Muslim countries, Ibn Battutah was sure of a warm welcome, a place to stay, and provisions for the next stage of his journey.

After his African journey, Ibn Battutah seems to have given up travelling. He was getting old and so, for the rest of his life, he lived quietly in Tangier, working as a judge and, perhaps, amusing the sultan and his courtiers with tales of his adventurous past.

The lighthouse at Alexandria was one of the wonders of the Ancient World. It had been built by the Ptolemies - Greek rulers of Egypt in the first century BC. It stood guard over the busy harbour, and warned shipping to steer clear of the dangerous coastline beyond. In Ibn Battutah's day, the lighthouse had been abandoned, but its ruins were still standing, and were a popular sight for travellers to visit.

At the start of his first long journey, Ibn Battutah was taken by local boatmen to see the ruins of the famous lighthouse at Alexandria in Egypt.

The 'Jornufa'

Ruy Gonzales de Clavijo, a diplomat in the service of King Henry of Castile, was writing his memoirs.
He was trying to describe an extraordinary creature, a 'jornufa', he had seen about three years before, but he wondered whether anyone would believe him.
'The animal,' he wrote 'has a body as big as a horse, but with an extremely long neck. Its forelegs are very much longer than the hind legs, and its hooves are divided like those of cattle ... The belly is white but the rest of the body is golden yellow, cross-marked with broad white bands ... The face, with the nose, resembles that of a deer ... the eyes are very large ... and the ears are like those of a horse, while near its ears are two small, round horns...'

Perhaps his readers would think that this 'jornufa' was just another imaginary monster. Travellers' tales were full of them. But Ruy Gonzales' 'jornufa' was real, not imaginary. It was a giraffe, and he was one of the few men in Spain ever to have seen one. Where had he met this wonderful creature?

It is not known where Sultan Faraj obtained the giraffe he sent to Timur. It may have been bred in captivity (many Muslim rulers had private zoos) in Egypt, where the climate would suit it. Certainly, it seems to have been tame, and its keepers obviously knew how to look after it well, otherwise it would not have survived the long journey to Samarkand.

In 1404 Ruy Gonzales had been sent as an ambassador to the court of Timur, the immensely powerful ruler of a large part of the Muslim world. It was many months' journey from Castile to Timur's capital city of Samarkand, and Ruy Gonzales had travelled part of the way with another group of diplomats, who were Muslims from the court of Sultan Faraj of Egypt.
Like Ruy Gonzales and his companions, the Egyptians had brought presents with them to give to Timur.
King Henry had sent specially trained falcons (Timur was fond of hunting) and valuable scarlet cloth.
But the sultan had instructed the Egyptian ambassador to deliver a far more precious gift: a giraffe and six ostriches. He had sent them to show how much he respected Timur, and because he hoped Timur would help him fight against his enemies.

Giraffes are normally found in the dry savannah grasslands of southern and central Africa. Their long necks enable them to eat the leaves from the topmost branches of trees, and their brown and yellow dappled coats provide camouflage to protect them from attack by lions and hyenas.

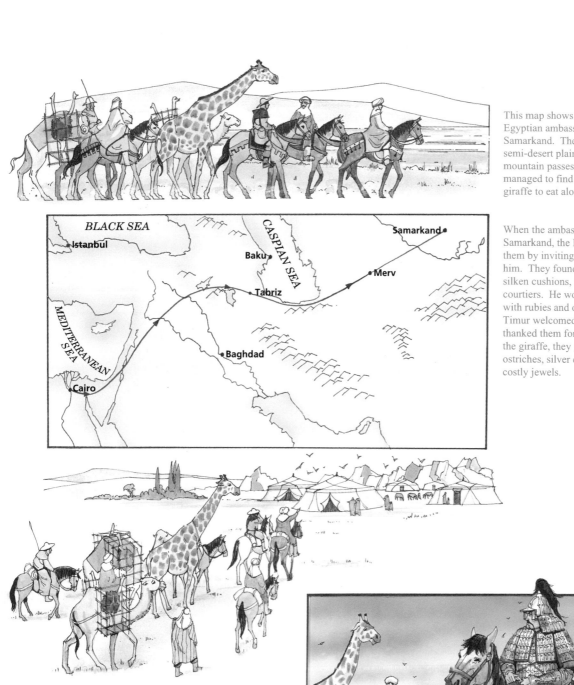

This map shows the route taken by the Egyptian ambassadors from Cairo to Samarkand. They travelled across dry, semi-desert plains and through snowy mountain passes. Somehow, they managed to find enough food for their giraffe to eat along the route.

When the ambassadors reached Samarkand, the Emperor Timur honoured them by inviting them to come and meet him. They found him sitting on a heap of silken cushions, attended by respectful courtiers. He wore a headdress decorated with rubies and other precious stones. Timur welcomed them courteously, and thanked them for their gifts. As well as the giraffe, they gave him several live ostriches, silver coins, rich fabrics and costly jewels.

BLACK SEA

Istanbul

CASPIAN SEA

Samarkand

Baku

Merv

Tabriz

MEDITERRANEAN SEA

Baghdad

Cairo

41

Timur's Empire

It is over 4,000 km from Cairo to Samarkand; the giraffe must have walked the entire distance. Unfortunately, it is not known how long the journey took. However, from Ruy Gonzales' memoirs, there are vivid descriptions of some of the places the travellers visited.

In Tehran, they were entertained to a magnificent feast by a local nobleman. They admired many beautiful buildings along the route, including the palace at Kesh, where Timur had been born. Gonzales wrote that it was 'so marvellously made that even the craftsmen of Paris, who are noted for their skill, would judge that which is done here to be of very fine workmanship'. In Samarkand itself, they marvelled at the great mosque, and at the bazaar, crowded with goods from eastern lands. They were also pleased to see people from many lands living side by side. Timur brought the best craftsmen from all the Muslim nations to Samarkand, and ordered them to work for him. Timur entertained the Egyptian and Spanish ambassadors to a great feast; afterwards, their presents, including the giraffe, were shown to admiring groups of courtiers and to other guests. It is quite likely that both ambassadors had further talks with Timur before setting off on their long journey home.

The Egyptian ambassador, whose name was Manglay Bugay, seems to have been an impressive character: 20 years after his visit, he (and the giraffe) were still remembered in Samarkand. In 1424 a Persian historian describing Manglay's visit wrote that he was 'endowed with rare qualities. He knew the entire Qur'an by heart, and he possessed the highest degree of eloquence, as well as several other talents, which made him the most pleasant man to converse with.' He was just one of the many Muslim travellers who explored the world at a time when their journeys demanded courage, daring, and above all, faith.

The Egyptian ambassadors were joined on their long journey to Samarkand by a party of Spanish diplomats. Together, they travelled through the lands occupied by nomadic Mongol peoples. Everywhere they went, the strange appearance of their giraffe attracted crowds of onlookers.

We know so much about the Egyptian sultan's gift of a giraffe to Timur because one of the Spanish diplomats wrote a detailed account of his meeting with the animal and its keepers, once he had returned to Spain.

He also described Timur's splendid capital city of Samarkand. Here is part of his description:
'The markets of Samarkand are amply stocked with merchandise imported from distant and foreign countries. From Russia and Tartary come leathers and linens, from China, silk stuffs that are the finest in the whole world ... Musk is imported from there, too, along with rubies and diamonds..., also pearls, lastly rhubarb and other spices.'

'From India are brought to Samarkand the lesser spices - the most costly ones - such as nutmegs and cloves and mace, with cinnamon... ginger and manna; all these with many other kinds that are never to be found in the markets of Alexandria.'

Glossary

Allah

The one and only God, creator and sustainer of the Universe.

Ambassadors

Trustworthy men sent to carry messages and to establish friendships between rulers of different countries.

Burnous

A loose, flowing robe with a hood.

Byzantine Empire

An empire ruled by Greek Christian kings, based in the city of Byzantium (also known as Constantinople, present-day Istanbul). The Byzantine empire included parts of Greece, Turkey, Albania, Georgia and Syria.

Caftan

A long, loose robe.

Casualties

People who have been injured.

Cocoon

The outer covering spun by a caterpillar to protect it while it changes into a moth.

Convoys

Large groups of people travelling together.

Cremation

The practice of burning a dead body rather than burying it. This practice is forbidden in Islam.

Crusades

A series of invasions of Jerusalem by Christian armies who wanted to capture the city from Islamic rule.

Eloquence

The art of speaking well.

Franks

An old name for the French people.

Hajji

A title of respect, meaning 'someone who has made the pilgrimage to Makkah.'

Islam

The state of yielding whole-heartedly to the guiding wisdom of Allah, therefore being at peace with oneself and other creatures through belief in the message brought by Prophet Muhammad ﷺ.

Khalifah

Literally, 'successor'. The title of the rulers of the Muslim world after the Prophet Muhammad ﷺ, who acted as guardians of the Islamic territories and as protectors of the Islamic faith.

Massacre

A brutal murder of a large number of people.

Monotonous

Boring.

Mosque

A place where Muslims pray.

Muhammad ﷺ	The prophet to whom Allah revealed the Qur'an, the seal of the prophets who brought messages from Allah. He lived in Arabia between about 570 and 632 CE.
Musk	A rare and very expensive ingredient used in perfumes. It comes from the musk-deer, which lives in China and Tibet.
Muslims	People who whole-heartedly yield to the guiding wisdom of Allah, therefore being at peace with themselves and other creatures, through belief in the message brought by the Prophet Muhammad ﷺ.
Nomads	People who move their homes, usually following good grazing for their herds of animals, rather than living a settled life in towns and villages.
Palestine	The lands around Jerusalem.
Parchment	Specially treated sheepskin, used to write on in the days before paper was widely available.
Porcelain	Fine, strong and beautiful 'china' - usually dishes, plates, bowls, cups etc. In the Middle Ages, only the Chinese people knew how to make it.
Properties	The structure of substances and their behaviour under different conditions. For example, one of the properties of water is that it will freeze when the temperature falls below 0° Celsius.
Prophet	A messenger sent by Allah to guide people to worship Allah, the One True God, and to teach them the right way to live. Many prophets have faced persecution for their beliefs, but, with Allah's help, have held firmly to their faith.
Qadi	A judge in the Shari'ah (Islamic law) court.
Shari'ah	Islamic law, covering all aspects of public and private behaviour.
Sheikh	A title of respect, often given to learned wise or elderly men.
Slavs	People who lived in the lands to the north of the Black Sea, and in southern Russia.
Sub-zero	Below freezing point.
Sultan	A ruler.
Synagogue	A place where Jewish people meet to pray.

Index

A

Aachen, 10
Abu Abbas, 11
Afghanistan, 34, 36
Africa, 8, 11, 20, 34, 38, 40
Al-Idrisi, 18, 20, 21
Al-Muqtadir, 12
Alexandria, 30, 32, 34, 35, 38, 43
Allah, 7, 16, 20, 22, 28, 32, 44
Arab, 10, 18, 22, 26, 30, 35, 36
Arabia, 7, 34, 35, 45
Arabian Sea, 34
Arabic, 10, 12, 20
Armenia, 28
Asia, 26, 30, 34
Azerbaijan, 28

B

Baghdad, 8, 10, 11, 12, 14, 16, 22, 34
Bangladesh 35
Basrah, 30
Black Sea, 26, 34, 45
Britain, 20
Bukhara, 26, 28, 34
Burhan al-Din, 32
Burma, 26, 35, 36
Byzantine, 22
Byzantine Empire, 8, 22, 26, 44
Byzantium, 19, 44

C

Cairo, 41, 42
Caspian Sea, 14, 16
Castile, 40
Central Asia, 26, 28, 34
Ceuta, 18
Charlemagne, 8, 10, 11
China, 7, 8, 12, 26, 32, 35, 36, 38, 43, 45
Chinese, 26, 28, 36, 45
Cordoba, 26
Cyprus, 19

D

Delhi, 35, 36

E

East Africa, 11, 34
East Indies, 12, 26
Egypt, 12, 30, 32, 34, 38, 40
Egyptian, 26, 40, 41, 42, 43
England, 24
Europe, 7, 10, 19, 22, 24, 25, 26, 30, 34

F

Farid al-Din, 32
Fez, 32
France, 24, 30
Franks, 8, 10, 22

G

Genoa, 10
Germany, 10, 12, 24
Gobi Desert, 28
Grand Canal, 30
Great Khan, 36
Greece, 19, 44
Greek, 38, 44

H

Himalayas, 34
Hangchow, 26
Harun al-Rashid, 8, 10, 11

I

Ibn Battutah, 32, 34, 35, 36, 38
Ibn Fadlan, 14, 16
Ibn Juzayy, 32, 34, 36
India, 7, 11, 12, 26, 30, 32, 35, 36, 43
Indian, 26, 30
Indian Ocean, 26, 36
Iran, 26
Isa ﷺ (Jesus), 22
Italy, 12, 19, 30

J

Java, 30
Jerusalem, 22, 24, 44, 45

IQRA TRUST

The IQRA TRUST provides clear, accurate and reliable information about Islam and the Muslim way of life.

EDUCATION

IQRA works with local education authorities, schools and teachers to provide information and training.

IQRA offers advice and guidance to encourage increased Muslim participation in the educational consultative process.

PUBLICATIONS

IQRA produces a wide range of publications, including:

- Guidance for teachers, social and health care workers and other professionals;

- Books and teaching materials for National Curriculum subjects.

INFORMATION TECHNOLOGY

IQRA holds an immense computerised database of information on Islamic subjects which is constantly being expanded and updated.

AUDIO-VISUAL MATERIALS

IQRA maintains the most comprehensive catalogue ever complied of films and videos and photographs on Islamic subjects.

If you would like to learn more about Islam and the work of IQRA, please contact:

IQRA TRUST, 24 Culross Street, London WlY 3HE

TRAVELLERS
AND EXPLORERS

First Published in 1992 by

IQRA TRUST
24 Culross Street
London WIY 3HE

Printed and bound in England

ISBN 1 85679 900 X